CHRISTMAS JOKE BOOK

 ## Book for Kids

This Book Belongs To:

_____

_____

THANK YOU...

Thank you for purchasing my book! Before you dive into your joke journey, please read the following:

HOW TO PLAY?

1 **Pick a Joke:** Take turns flipping through the book and picking a joke to read aloud.

2 **Guess the Punchline:** Before revealing the answer, let others guess the punchline.

3 **Rate the Laughter:** After hearing the joke, rate it on a scale of 1-5 Christmas candy for how funny it is!

4 **Friendly Competition:** Keep track of who guesses the most punchlines correctly and declare them the "Christmas Jokester."

A CUTE GIFT INSIDE

Enjoy The Gift Inside

We genuinely care about your child's experience and want them to enjoy every moment of creativity with this Christmas Try Not To Laugh Challenge. As a token of our appreciation, we've prepared a special gift just for them!

Their happiness and satisfaction mean everything to us. As a thank you for choosing our book, visit the Gift Link to claim their special surprise!

https://bit.ly/*********

Full Link on Page 34

STAY BLESSED..

TRY NOT TO LAUGH CHALLENGE

What do you call an elf who sings?

A wrapper!

Why is it so cold at Christmas?

Because it's Decem-brrrr!

TRY NOT TO LAUGH CHALLENGE

Why did the Christmas tree go to the barber?

It needed a little trim-mas!

What do you call Santa when he takes a break?

Santa Pause

TRY NOT TO LAUGH CHALLENGE

What do reindeer say before they tell a joke?

This one's gonna sleigh you!

Why did the ornament go to school?

To become a little brighter.

TRY NOT TO LAUGH CHALLENGE

Why did the snowman call a doctor?

He felt a little chilly.

What do you call a present that tells jokes?

A pun-derful gift!

TRY NOT TO LAUGH CHALLENGE

Why did the ornament go to the gym?

To get a little tree-mendous workout!

Why was the snowman's dog barking at the Christmas tree?

He thought it was a bark!

TRY NOT TO LAUGH CHALLENGE

How do you decorate a reindeer's house?

With rein-bows!

What's a Christmas tree's favorite candy?

Orna-mints

TRY NOT TO LAUGH CHALLENGE

What do you call a present that's not very good?

A "re-gift"!

What did one gift say to the other gift?

"You're a wrap!"

Why wouldn't the Christmas tree stand up?

It had no legs

What do you get when Santa plays detective?

Santa clues!

TRY NOT TO LAUGH CHALLENGE

How do snowmen get around?

By riding an "icicle"

What do you get if you cross a snowman and a dog?

Frostbite!

TRY NOT TO LAUGH CHALLENGE

What do you call Santa when he loses his pants?

Saint Knickerless!

What do you call a cat on Christmas morning?

Sandy Claws!

TRY NOT TO LAUGH CHALLENGE

What's red and white and falls down chimneys?

Santa klutz

What's as big as a Christmas tree but lighter than a feather?

Its shadow

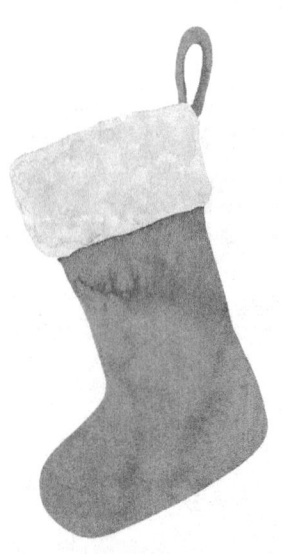

TRY NOT TO LAUGH CHALLENGE

What do you get if you cross a snowman and a vampire?

Frostbite!

What's Santa's favorite snack?

Claus-tard

TRY NOT TO LAUGH CHALLENGE

What do sheep say to each other during the holidays?

Merry Christmas to ewe!

What did one Christmas tree say to another?

You light up my life!!

What did one Christmas ornament say to the other ornament?

"I like hanging out with you!"

What did one snowman say to the other snowman?

"Do you smell carrots?"

TRY NOT TO LAUGH CHALLENGE

What do you call a snowman party?

A snowball

Why did the gingerbread cookie go to the doctor?

Because it was feeling crumby

TRY NOT TO LAUGH CHALLENGE

What does an elf study in school?

The elfabet

Where does a snowman keep his money?

in a snow bank

TRY NOT TO LAUGH CHALLENGE

What did one Christmas tree say to the other Christmas tree?

Lighten up

What is Santa's dog's name?

Santa paws

TRY NOT TO LAUGH CHALLENGE

Why do mummies like Christmas so much?

Because of all the wrapping

How do sheep wish each other happy holidays?

Marry Christmas to ewe

TRY NOT TO LAUGH CHALLENGE

What kind of music do elves like?

Wrap music

Why did the little boy bring his Christmas tree to the hair salon?

It needs a little trim

TRY NOT TO LAUGH CHALLENGE

Why do you think everyone loves Frosty the Snowman?

Because he is COOL!

What did Adam say to Eve the day before Christmas?

Its Christmas, Eve!

TRY NOT TO LAUGH CHALLENGE

What comes at the end of Christmas?

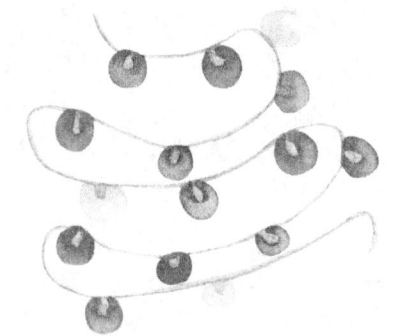

The letter's

In which year does New Year's Day come before Christmas?

Every year

25

TRY NOT TO LAUGH CHALLENGE

What do the monkeys sing on Christmas Eve?

The jungle bells

What are the photos of elves called?

The elfies

TRY NOT TO LAUGH CHALLENGE

Why was the snowman shopping for carrots?

He wanted a new nose

What is the most competitive season?

Win-ter!

TRY NOT TO LAUGH CHALLENGE

How much did Santa pay for his sleigh?

Nothing, it was on the house!

Which one of Santa's reindeer has the best moves?

Dancer

TRY NOT TO LAUGH CHALLENGE

How does Santa Claus keep track of every fireplace he has already visited?

Well, he keeps a log

What do elves do after school?

Their gnome work

TRY NOT TO LAUGH CHALLENGE

What do you get if you cross a snowman and a vampire?

Frostbite!

What did one ornament say to another ornament?

I'm really hanging around this tree alot!

TRY NOT TO LAUGH CHALLENGE

What did Santa say at the start of the race?

Ready.set.ho ho ho!

What is it called when Santa takes a break?

A santa pause

TRY NOT TO LAUGH CHALLENGE

What do snowmen eat for lunch?

Ice bergers

What do you call a greedy elf?

Elfish

TRY NOT TO LAUGH CHALLENGE

Why was the Christmas tree so bad at knitting?

It kept dropping its needles!

How do snow get around?

They ride an ICICLE

TRY NOT TO LAUGH CHALLENGE

What did the stamp say to the christmas card?

Stick with me and we'll go places

What do you call Santa when he takes a break?

Santa pause

STAY BLESSED

Enjoy The Gift Below!

https://bit.ly/ 3GGWoS8

Tap this link in the browser and enjoy!
If you loved the book and the idea give us your honest review.

TRY NOT TO LAUGH CHALLENGE

What does a grumpy sheep say when his friends tell him Merry Christmas?

BAAAAA Humbug!

Why wouldn't the Christmas tree stand up?

It had no legs

TRY NOT TO LAUGH CHALLENGE

How do you scare a snowman?

Grab a hairdryer

Who is never hungry at Christmas?

The turkey.he's alway's stuffed

TRY NOT TO LAUGH CHALLENGE

What did one snowman say to the other snowman?

Do you smell carrots?

What comes at the end of Christmas Day?

The letter "y"

TRY NOT TO LAUGH CHALLENGE

What do you get if you eat a Christmas decoration?

Tinsel-itis

What do you call an obnoxious reindeer?

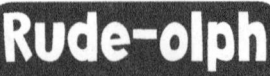

Rude-olph

TRY NOT TO LAUGH CHALLENGE

Why is it getting hard to buy advent calendars?

Their days are numbered

What do you call a broke santa?

Saint nickel-less

TRY NOT TO LAUGH CHALLENGE

What does the gingerbread man put on his bed?

Cookie sheets

How does a sheep say merry christmas?

Fleece navidad

TRY NOT TO LAUGH CHALLENGE

Why didn't Rudolph get a good report card?

Because he went down in history

What is it called when a snowman has a temper tantrum?

A meltdown

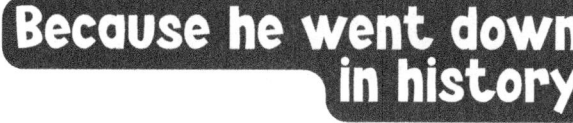

TRY NOT TO LAUGH CHALLENGE

Why are Christmas trees so bad at sewing?

They always drop their needles

Why was the gingerbread man robbed?

Because of all his dough

TRY NOT TO LAUGH CHALLENGE

What's the difference between Santa and a knight?

One slays the dragon, the other drags the sleigh.

What do you get if Santa goes down the chimney when a fire is lit?

Crisp kringle

TRY NOT TO LAUGH CHALLENGE

How do you know when Santa's around?

You can sense his presents

What falls at the North Pole and never gets hurt?

Snow

TRY NOT TO LAUGH CHALLENGE

How much did Santa pay for his sleigh?

nothing. It was on the house.

What do you call Santa Claus with unfolded clothes?

kris wrinkle.

TRY NOT TO LAUGH CHALLENGE

Why was the snowman looking through the carrots?

he was picking his nose.

why did the gingerbread man go to the doctor?

because he was feeling crumby.

TRY NOT TO LAUGH CHALLENGE

Why do basketball players love gingerbread cookies?

because they can dunk them.

What do snowmen take when the sun gets too hot?

a chill pill.

TRY NOT TO LAUGH CHALLENGE

What do you get if you cross a snowman and a vampire?

Frostbite!

What did one ornament say to another ornament?

I'm really hanging around this tree a lot!

TRY NOT TO LAUGH CHALLENGE

What do elves use to take notes in school?

Elf-abet soup!

Why was the math book sad during the holidays?

It had too many problems!

TRY NOT TO LAUGH CHALLENGE

What do sheep say to each other during the holidays?

Merry Christmas

Merry Christmas to ewe!

How does a snowman get around?

By riding an "icicle"!

TRY NOT TO LAUGH CHALLENGE

What did one Christmas tree say to another?

"You light up my life!"

Why was the snowman looking through the carrots?

He was picking his nose!

TRY NOT TO LAUGH CHALLENGE

Why did the ornament go to school?

Because it wanted to be a "smarty ball"!

What do you call an elf who sings?

A wrapper!

TRY NOT TO LAUGH CHALLENGE

What do snowmen eat for lunch?

Icebergers!

What did Santa say to the smoker?

Please don't smoke—it's bad for my elf!

TRY NOT TO LAUGH CHALLENGE

Why did the Christmas tree go to the barber?

It needed a trim!

What's a snowman's favorite game?

Freeze tag!

TRY NOT TO LAUGH CHALLENGE

What do you call a reindeer that tells jokes?

A "comet"-ian!

What do you give a train for Christmas?

Tracks of land!

TRY NOT TO LAUGH CHALLENGE

What do you give an elephant for Christmas?

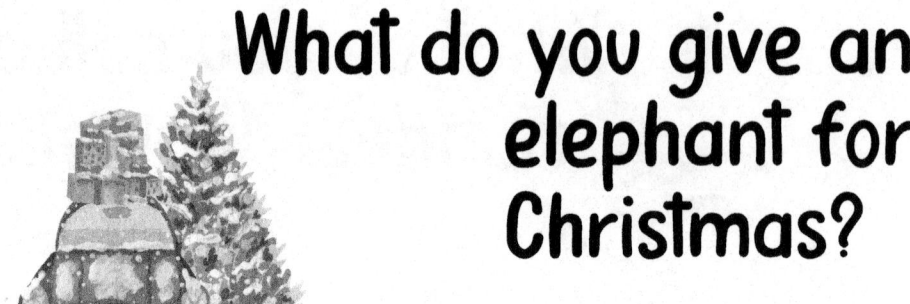

A trunk full of presents!

Why did the gift wrap itself?

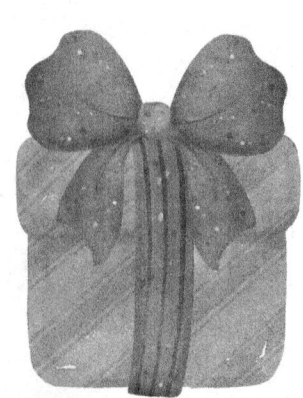

It wanted to be a surprise!

TRY NOT TO LAUGH CHALLENGE

Why was Santa's helper depressed?

He had low elf-esteem.

What do reindeer hang on their Christmas trees?

Horn-aments!

TRY NOT TO LAUGH CHALLENGE

What do reindeer use to dry themselves after a bath?

A deer's towel!

Why did the snowman turn yellow?

Because he saw the snowblower coming!

TRY NOT TO LAUGH CHALLENGE

What do you call a snowman party?

A snowball!

Why did the turkey go to the North Pole?

To get chilly!

TRY NOT TO LAUGH CHALLENGE

What do you get if you cross a snowman and a baker?

Frosting!

Why did the ornament go to the doctor?

It felt a little shattered!

TRY NOT TO LAUGH CHALLENGE

What did the gingerbread man use to fix his house?

Icing and gumdrops!

Why did the snowman bring a broom to the Christmas party?

To sweep the ladies off their feet!

TRY NOT TO LAUGH CHALLENGE

How does a snowman stay cool?

By standing next to the fan!

Why did the snowman call the weather report?

He wanted to know if there was a chance of frostbite!

TRY NOT TO LAUGH CHALLENGE

What do snowmen eat for breakfast?

Frosted flakes!

Why was the snowman looking sad?

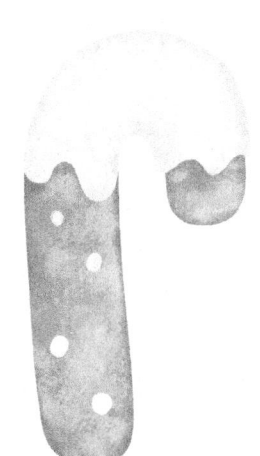

He had a meltdown!

TRY NOT TO LAUGH CHALLENGE

What did the Christmas tree say to the ornament?

"Quit hanging around and get to work!"

What do snowmen do on weekends?

Chill out!

TRY NOT TO LAUGH CHALLENGE

Why did the ornament go to the dentist?

It needed a filling!

Why did the snowman call the weather station?

He wanted to know if he should wear an extra scarf!

TRY NOT TO LAUGH CHALLENGE

Why did the snowflake go to school?

To get a little flake education!

What do you call an elf who runs away from Santa's workshop?

A rebel without a Claus!

TRY NOT TO LAUGH CHALLENGE

How does a snowman greet another snowman?

Ice to meet you!

What do snowmen wear on their heads?

Ice caps!

TRY NOT TO LAUGH CHALLENGE

Why don't reindeer like to play cards in the wild?

Too many cheetahs!

Why was the reindeer so good at making jokes?

He had a great sense of rein!

TRY NOT TO LAUGH CHALLENGE

Why did the gift go to therapy?

It had too many unwrapped emotions!

What's the best Christmas present your parents ever gave you?

A warm hug.

TRY NOT TO LAUGH CHALLENGE

What do you call a snowman with a sunburn?

A puddle!

What's a snowman's favorite type of gift?

Frostbite-sized presents!

TRY NOT TO LAUGH CHALLENGE

Why did the family play hide-and-seek?

It's the best way to find joy!

What's a snowman's favorite kind of music?

Anything that's cool!

TRY NOT TO LAUGH CHALLENGE

What do you call Santa when he starts a podcast?

Kris Talkin'!

Why did the Christmas cookie go to school?

It wanted to be a smartie!

TRY NOT TO LAUGH CHALLENGE

What do you call a snowman with a smartphone?

A chill-texter!

Why did the elf bring a ladder to the bar?

He heard the drinks were on the house!

TRY NOT TO LAUGH CHALLENGE

What do reindeer use to style their fur?

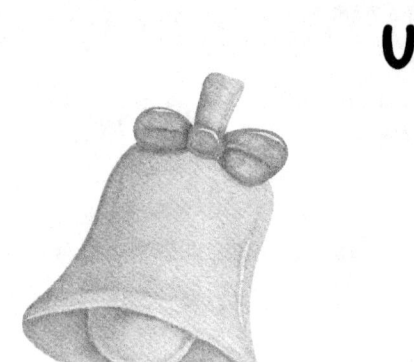

Gel-bells!

Why was the present so quiet?

Because it was gift-wrapped in silence!

TRY NOT TO LAUGH CHALLENGE

What's Santa's favorite workout?

The sleigh press!

What game do elves play at recess?

Freeze tag!

TRY NOT TO LAUGH CHALLENGE

Why was Rudolph's report card wet?

Because he had too many snow "flakes"!

What do you call a grumpy snowman?

A flurry of attitude!

TRY NOT TO LAUGH CHALLENGE

What happens when elves get cold?

They just "chill" out!

What's an elf's favorite holiday story?

The Nutcracker—because it cracks them up!

TRY NOT TO LAUGH CHALLENGE

What do you call an elf who tells the truth?

Honest Abe-elf!

Why did the elf cross the road?

To get to the "jingle" side!

TRY NOT TO LAUGH CHALLENGE

What's an elf's favorite animal?

Rein-deer!

What do elves use to fix toys?

Glue sticks and candy canes!

TRY NOT TO LAUGH CHALLENGE

What do you call an elf who loves to sing?

A carol-elf!

What's an elf's favorite kind of joke?

Pun-derful ones!

TRY NOT TO LAUGH CHALLENGE

Why are elves so good at math?

They're great at "toy"-tals!

What's an elf's favorite classroom rule?

Be your "elf"!

TRY NOT TO LAUGH CHALLENGE

What do elves say when they're surprised?

"Snow way!"

Why did the elf bring a ladder to the workshop?

To help the toys reach new heights!

TRY NOT TO LAUGH CHALLENGE

What's an elf's favorite drink?

Hot "coco-elf"!

What kind of pet do elves like?

Christmas corgis!

TRY NOT TO LAUGH CHALLENGE

What's an elf's favorite game at recess?

Snow-and-seek!

Why are elves good at riddles?

They're always thinking on their little feet!

TRY NOT TO LAUGH CHALLENGE

How do elves cheer each other up?

They tell "tree"-mendous jokes!

What's an elf's favorite subject in school?

Sp-elf-ing!

TRY NOT TO LAUGH CHALLENGE

Why did the elf sit on the shelf?

He wanted to be the center of "elf"-tention!

Why did the ornament start lifting weights?

It wanted to hang with the big baubles.

TRY NOT TO LAUGH CHALLENGE

Why did the ornament go to the party?

It wanted to hang with the big baubles.

Why did the snowflake apply for a job?

It wanted to make a flurry of income.

TRY NOT TO LAUGH CHALLENGE

Why did the candy cane get promoted?

It had a sweet attitude.

Why did Santa bring string?

To tie up loose ends!

Why was the gingerbread late?

He got caught in a jam.

Why did the elf bring a spoon to work?

He heard it was a stirring job.

TRY NOT TO LAUGH CHALLENGE

Why did the Christmas light feel dim?

It lost its spark.

Why was the reindeer always calm?

He had great "rein" control.

TRY NOT TO LAUGH CHALLENGE

Why didn't the tree talk back?

It didn't want to get chopped.

Why did the present stay unopened?

It wasn't ready to come out of its shell.

TRY NOT TO LAUGH CHALLENGE

Why did the tinsel feel important?

It always knew how to shine under pressure.

Why did the snowman stay cool?

He had a chill personality.

TRY NOT TO LAUGH CHALLENGE

Why did the elf skip school?

He had too many wrapping assignments.

Why was the sleigh so noisy?

It had too many bells and whistles.

TRY NOT TO LAUGH CHALLENGE

Why did the present blush?

It was caught under the mistletoe.

Why didn't the tree go to the party?

It didn't want to get lit.

TRY NOT TO LAUGH CHALLENGE

Why did Santa avoid the bakery?

He didn't want to crumble under pressure.

Why was the candy cane always invited?

It was a real sweet talker.

TRY NOT TO LAUGH CHALLENGE

Why did the Christmas card feel ignored?

It got lost in the shuffle.

Why did the fireplace feel proud?

It always sparked joy.

TRY NOT TO LAUGH CHALLENGE

Why did the snow globe apply for a raise?

It was tired of being shaken up.

Why did the star join the band?

It wanted to shine on stage.

TRY NOT TO LAUGH CHALLENGE

Why did the wreath break up with the door?

It felt used.

Why was the nutcracker so serious?

He couldn't crack a smile.

TRY NOT TO LAUGH CHALLENGE

Why did the wrapping paper go to therapy?

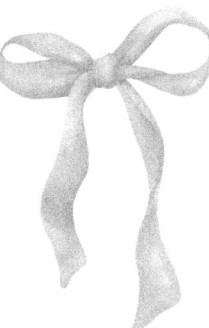

It was feeling all torn up.

Why did the gingerbread man apply for a job?

He needed the dough.

TRY NOT TO LAUGH CHALLENGE

Why didn't the snowflake show up?

It flaked out.

Why was the elf so calm?

He knew how to keep his shelf control.

TRY NOT TO LAUGH CHALLENGE

Why did the mistletoe start gossiping?

It liked to stir up kisses and drama.

Why did the ornament break up with the tree?

It needed space to hang out alone.

TRY NOT TO LAUGH CHALLENGE

Why was the Christmas light so moody?

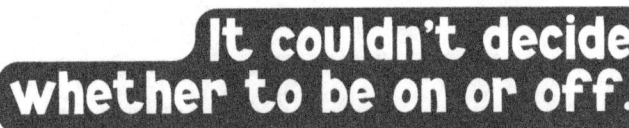

It couldn't decide whether to be on or off.

Why did the snowman call in sick?

He felt a bit runny.

TRY NOT TO LAUGH CHALLENGE

What do you call a sneaky Christmas pie?

A mince-chief!

How do reindeer cheer for their team?

They give a big hoof-hooray!

TRY NOT TO LAUGH CHALLENGE

What did one snowflake say to another?

You're one in a blizzard!

Why doesn't Santa ever get sick?

Because he has private elf care!

TRY NOT TO LAUGH CHALLENGE

Why did the Christmas lights break up?

They couldn't handle the current situation.

What kind of photos do elves love to take?

 Elf-ies!

Printed in Dunstable, United Kingdom